The Fungi Phenomenon

A Coloring Journey Through Mushrooms

This book belong to

____

____

Preface

Welcome to "The Fungi Phenomenon: A Coloring Journey Through Mushrooms"! This coloring book is designed for adults who appreciate the natural beauty and complexity of mushrooms, and who enjoy the therapeutic benefits of coloring.

Throughout history, mushrooms have captured our imaginations and inspired a sense of wonder and curiosity. From their intricate shapes and textures, to their diverse colors and patterns, mushrooms are fascinating organisms that are essential to our ecosystem.

In this coloring book, you'll embark on a journey through the world of mushrooms, with each page featuring a different species or variety for you to color and admire. Whether you prefer the bright and bold hues of the fly agaric, or the delicate and intricate shapes of the coral mushroom, there's something here for everyone.

But coloring isn't just a fun and relaxing activity - it's also been shown to have numerous health benefits. Coloring has been found to reduce stress, anxiety, and even symptoms of depression. It can also help to improve focus, concentration, and fine motor skills.

So, whether you're an experienced artist or just looking for a new way to unwind, we hope that "The Fungi Phenomenon" will provide you with hours of enjoyment and relaxation. Get ready to explore the fascinating world of mushrooms, one color at a time!

Mushrooms are a type of fungi that are found in a wide range of environments, from forests and grasslands to deserts and even in the depths of the ocean. They are unique organisms that play a vital role in many ecosystems, helping to break down organic matter and recycle nutrients.

There are over 14,000 known species of mushrooms, with new species being discovered every year. They come in a variety of shapes, sizes, and colors, with some being highly sought after for their culinary or medicinal properties.

Mushrooms have been used for centuries in traditional medicine, with some species being known for their anti-inflammatory, immune-boosting, and anti-cancer properties. They are also a popular ingredient in many cuisines around the world, with species like the button mushroom and shiitake being staples in many dishes.

However, not all mushrooms are safe to eat, and some can even be deadly. It's important to have a thorough understanding of the different species and their properties before consuming them.

Despite their importance to the ecosystem and human health, mushrooms remain a mysterious and fascinating organism. They continue to inspire wonder and curiosity among scientists, artists, and nature enthusiasts alike, and we continue to learn more about their complexity and beauty with each passing year.

NIP
BIK
TNG

Poisonous